Fire Safety

- If your house catches on fire, go to the nearest neighbor to call 911 for help. If you are on a cellphone, give the operator your exact address and stay outside.
- If you are inside a closed room, feel the door before you open it to see if it is hot.
- Smoke is dangerous. Smoke rises, so get on your hands and knees and crawl to the nearest exit away from the fire.
- Most families have an exit plan and a specific meeting place outside their homes in case of a fire, and they practice this plan.

Fire Safety

- Keep lighters and matches away from children.
- Teach children how to call for emergency assistance.
- If your clothing catches on fire, it is important not to run.
- To put out the fire: stop, drop and roll.
- Keep young children safely away from space heaters.
- Practice the stop, drop and roll scenario with children.

Woodstoves and Fireplaces

- Be sure the stove or fireplace is installed properly. Woodstoves should have adequate clearance from flammable surfaces and proper floor support and protection.
- Only use seasoned wood and never use green wood, artificial logs or trash.
- Do not use flammable liquids to start or accelerate any fire.

Internet and Cyber Safety

- Do not give out personal information such as your name, telephone number or address. Do not give out information about your parents.
- Tell your parents immediately if you come across anything that makes you feel uncomfortable.
- Do not agree to get together with anyone you meet online.
- Do not send anyone a picture of yourself.
- Do not share your Internet password with anyone other than your parents.
- Talk to your parents about the house rules for using the Internet.

Match the Definition
Client chooses words and definitions

1) Hospital _____

2) Nurse _____

3) Firefighter _____

4) Exercise _____

5) Vaccination _____

6) Vegetables _____

7) Police Officer _____

8) Ambulance _____

A) Bodily activity that enhances or maintains physical fitness and overall health.

B) An institution for health care providing treatment for the hurt and ill.

C) A person employed to extinguish or prevent fires.

D) A shot to produce immunity from a disease.

E) The edible parts of plants.

F) A person generally responsible for apprehending criminals, prevention and detection of crime.

G) A vehicle for transporting ill or injured people.

H) A person who is responsible—along with other health care professionals—for the treatment, safety, and recovery of ill/injured people.

ANSWERS
1) B 2) H 3) C 4) A 5) D 6) E 7) F 8) G

5

Playground Safety

- Make sure adult supervision is present at the playground.
- Guide children to play on age-appropriate equipment.
- Survey the play area and make sure it is free of apparent hazards.
- Check the playground surface for cushioned surfacing beneath equipment and its fall areas.

Playground Safety

- Always wear a bike helmet.
- Walk your bike through intersections.
- Avoid peak sun intensity hours and always wear sunscreen when playing outside.

After School Safety

- When walking home from school, always go straight home, unless your mom, dad or babysitter gives you permission to stop and play.
- Always let your mom or dad or babysitter know if you're going to be late.
- When going home after school, NEVER accept a ride from a stranger.

School Bus Safety

- Have a safe place to wait for your bus, away from traffic and the street.
- Stay away from the bus until it comes to a complete stop and the driver signals you to enter.
- When being dropped off, exit the bus and walk ten giant steps away from the bus.

Health Word Search

```
I M M U N I Z A T I O N
E C N Z Z V L G E R M S
X J O V L A T I P S O H
E N I E S P E F N W F O
R G T S M A K S M R R T
C T A A K C F R R G D S
I Z N E I Q C E H U R D
S W I S M K K E T O N Z
E K C I Q K A L T Y M R
W R C D W L R C V N M N
M K A H T B O P B T K Q
L Z V H M D X L T K M M
```

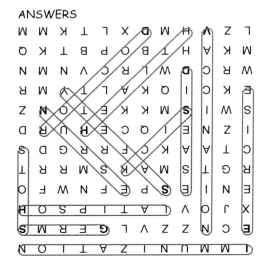

ANSWERS

WORD BANK

disease immunization
doctor nurse
exercise safety
germs shots
health sick
hospital vaccination

Weather Safety

- As soon as you hear thunder or see lightning, you should go indoors.
- Never stand under or go near a tree during a thunderstorm.
- Metal and water are two of the best conductors of electricity. Stay out of the water and stay away from metal buildings and fences during a storm.
- If you see a tornado or hear a tornado warning, get underground if possible or go into a well-constructed building. Stay away from windows and head toward inside walls.
- If you're caught outdoors during a thunderstorm, get to low ground, and avoid hills and mountaintops.

Walking in your town

- Never go into a public restroom alone.
- Never play too close to the curb or in the street.
- Never wait alone.

Swimming Safety

- Never leave children alone in or near the pool or beach, even for a second.
- At the pool or beach, make sure that anyone watching your children knows CPR and is able to rescue a child if needed.
- Young children often swallow the pool water which may be dirty, resulting in a higher risk of getting sick.

Water Safety

- Children should never swim around anchored boats, in motorboat lanes or where people are water skiing. Also, they should never swim during electrical storms.
- In order to avoid spinal injuries from diving, swimmers should not dive in shallow areas of lakes, ponds, beaches, streams or pools where the depth of the water is not known. Do not dive into above-ground pools.

Crossword Puzzle

Fill in the blanks with these healthy foods.

WORD BANK: bread, cheese, eggs, fats, ~~fish~~, fruit, meat, milk, oils, rice, yogurt.

Answers from page 20

Know it is OK to say NO!

- Have a secret password if a friend or relative picks you up at school.
- Know that it's ok to yell "NO" if a stranger offers you a ride home.
- If someone tries to force you into an automobile, scream, kick, bite and yell "NO, NO, NO"!

Don't Talk to Strangers

- Do not give directions to or get help from a stranger.
- Never accept a gift or a ride from a stranger.
- Never go in a stranger's car for candy or to look at a puppy.
- Never be fooled by a stranger or give him your name.

Personal Car Safety

- Never stick your head, arms, or legs out of the automobile while it's moving.
- Always wait for the car to come to a complete stop before approaching.

Personal Car Safety

- Most car crashes that seriously hurt people happen when the car is going 10 miles per hour faster than the speed limit.
- Always buckle your seat belt and use both lap and shoulder belts.

Find the 6 differences in these two pictures.

Answers on page 15

HOME SAFETY

Do not take any medicine without adult supervision and ask when it's time to take medication.
Always ask about an item if you are unsure whether or not it is safe to touch, taste, eat, or smell before handling the item.

Home Safety: Poison and Medications

- Keep the National Poison Control Center hotline number on each phone: 1-800-222-1222
- Keep all cleaning products, medicines and vitamins out of children's reach.

Safe Cooking and Fire Safety Habits

- Don't leave food unattended on the stove.
- Keep dangling clothing away from burners.
- Keep appliances clean and free of grease and crumbs.
- Keep curtains and other combustibles away from stove.

Don't Talk to Strangers

- It is not safe to have your name on your shirt.
- If a stranger approaches you and you think you are in danger, run away and yell "FIRE" as loudly as you can.
- Never believe a stranger who says your mom or dad sent them to pick you up.